GILDED

Rachel Orange

BookLeaf
Publishing
India | USA | UK

Presentation by *BookLeaf Publishing*

Web: www.bookleafpub.com

E-mail: info@bookleafpub.com

ISBN: 9789358738742

First edition 2021

PREFACE

Dreams are much like you

When you want to be a writer, one of your first big dreams is to get your book published. What isn't always said, however (and can never be said too often), is how much you'll crash around before finding yourself. Heaven knows I've done plenty of that, not to mention the feedback loop of writing stuff, putting it out there, taking in critiques, and applying those critiques. In the end, you may have something completely different from what you imagined.

Flashy scenes without meaning

If you say or read a word enough times, it temporarily loses all meaning. Writing can be like that sometimes. Regardless of how your story initially forms, you can lose yourself in the mechanical aspects and you almost forget what you're really doing here. This is even more evident with poetry: always remembering to show, not tell, as you try to do more with even fewer words.

And gone by morning

Besides beginning, one of the hardest parts of any big project is deciding when it's done, especially if it's your first one. Then I remember Paul Valery, and how every piece of art may well be a victim of abandonment. There can always be more, but one step back is worth more than taking the ten more forward that might not take you anywhere.

ACKNOWLEDGEMENTS

I would like to thank everyone at Bookleaf Publishing, especially Aarti, Gin Hangshing, and Shivangi Verma, who presented me with the opportunity to publish my poetry. Without them, this book would not exist. I hope you all know that you helped me take the first step in accomplishing my dreams.

I would also like to thank my parents for, among countless other things, always encouraging my interest in the arts and allowing me the privilege of going to college. I love you both so much, but I can't thank either of you enough. I hope you like my poems too.

For Ben

1.

Did you see potential

In me alone

Or in my silence

And compliance

2. CHANGE

A day ages me by years

Still more will pass before I see you

While you remain

Outliving a shell

3. HUNGER

The eyes betray

What we wish to conceal

4. BLUE AND BROWN

How strange that your eyes

Lend themselves to a different kind of purity

Never does your gaze seem clouded

They scream the loudest in your silence

Yet their offer of a labyrinth does not cease

And I don't want to find the exit

Meanwhile, here I am

A jealously guarded innocent, pretending to play with fire

That wouldn't know the first thing about burning

Yet snug in my head are two dying coals

Shifty, staring, searching

Waiting

5. PRIDE

"Let him who is without sin cast the first stone!"

And so the crowd

Became a rabble

And traded blows

From throwing stones

6. UNREQUITED

I carry a song no one has heard

In the notation lies "accompaniment"

Yet no voice rings clear

And if you allowed for a duet

Would our burdens be lifted?

Mine would be, this I know

But you, ever the soloist

Need no returned support

So I, bred for this and little else, am burdensome

Yet more verses are written

And melodies deaden

7. BACKSPACE

Backspace

Pause again

Where was I going with this?

They've already lost interest

Pause again

I begin again

They've already lost interest

Too wordy, they're thinking, so unclear

I begin again

Interrupting, "I wasn't finished."

Too wordy, they're thinking, so unclear

They ignore me

Interrupting, "I wasn't finished."

A pair of eyes shifts politely to me

They ignore me

They've already lost interest

A pair of eyes shifts politely to me

Where was I going with this?

They've already lost interest

Backspace

8. JOIN THEM

Only your first breath is your own

All else belongs to those around you

And no, my dear, you're not alone

It happened to your forefathers too

Given life in all its glory, yet fated

To die, my dear, just like you

Forgotten figures, their pictures faded

And yours will sit among them too

9. FATE

Everyone is picture-perfect

And so we shall be

10. FORGOTTEN

You disappeared

Without a word

And forgot everything

11. ONE LONG DREAM

A happy couple woke you

A mirror, in turn, woke me

Screaming robbed us of our dream

But the veil was lifted in silence

12. SUNDOWN

Sunlight filled your eyes before

Colors come and go with time

For the first time

And the last time

At sundown

The tapestry fades to grey

Disassembled

To be resewn tomorrow

But tomorrow never comes

The colors are gone

You ask who I am

I can't make you remember

13. GILDED

Dreams are much like you

Flashy scenes without meaning

And gone by morning

14. WHAT FRIENDS DO

Long since vanished

Without a word

You forgot everything

15. THE POSTMAN

In the week my family and I anticipated the postman's arrival,

My son told me that, when I received the delivery, I was to sign my name.

"He won't know who you are until he has your name," he said.

"He's forgetful like that. He makes a lot of deliveries every day."

The soft knock prompting the walk to the front door was a long one.

My wife caught my hand before mine was on the doorknob, and I looked at her.

About fifty years welled up in her eyes, and forty-five years immobilized my son.

"I think he's here on time," I said.

"No, he's a day early," murmured my wife, "he can come back tomorrow.'

"No, dad's right," said my son, "he said he'd be here in a week."

As the two people I loved the most fretted and argued in whispers,

I took from the postman's hands what was intended for me.

"Beautiful day, isn't it?" He asked

"Yes, it is," I replied, "peaceful."

"Now, if you could just sign your name, sir."

My name was one of many on his list.

None of this was special.

"I'll give you until midnight," said the postman, "but after that, I'll have to come for you."

"No, I'm ready now," I replied.

"They're just arguing about when you were supposed to get here. I've been expecting you for a week."

What I had been given was a large box

With a shovel and white lilies inside.

16. TOUCH

How bold of your hand

To replace your timid tongue

When you don't know mine

17. SILENCE

Solemnly bowing

Strangled into submission

By a holy noose

18. BUTTERFLY

He never tore its wings off

If he did, it wasn't in any pain

And if it was, it will die anyway

And if he didn't know that, it's not his fault

And if it is, he didn't mean to

And if he did, it deserved it

19. GREED

A pleasant surprise

Bound for me in silk ribbons

Avarice forced my hand

I devour my gift

20. AUTOPSY

I attended your autopsy, numbly listening

To the pathologist, leisurely listing

Your pristine organs, bones, and all

Then out your brain fell from your skull

Red brought with it silence and shock

A pungence wafted from the flood

That made even the pathologist balk

A brain in pieces, near-dissolved to blood

The pathologist, at last, concluded

Mostly normal, save the head

Cause of death till now eluded

Poisoned slowly, then left for dead

21. STONE

Admired so is stoicism

To be the stone that divides the river

But in the time you stand your ground

The erosion and reshaping shows

Until the river reflects dichotomy

22. NOSFERATU

Watching from shadows

Awaiting invitation

Fresh prey within reach

23. BLOSSOM

The sapling blossoms in the yard

Thin branches bearing tiny flowers

I thought then of your first hours

You were born without a heart

The sapling took root over you

You shared a name and birthday

And on what would have been your first

There were blossoms on that Spring day

The years roll by, the sapling grows

Your sister turns seven

Old wounds close

Under branches reaching up to heaven

24. KISS

Heat filled that summer

Heat that has not burned since then

For no kiss was his

25. SUMMER

We had nothing to do

But race the clouds

And stain our clothes

From rolling in grass

All we had

Were bicycles

And bare feet

We didn't care

Our whole world

Was just one street

And in fading daylight

We fled from the night

26. BLOOD

A Pollock copy

Unceremoniously

Done up all in red

27. NO FACE

I am one of many in a masquerade

Music almost drowns the sound

Of excited chatter from my guests

Each daring the other to approach me

They speak to the mask

In all its intricate perfection

This one is my favorite

It's their favorite too

Under my mask

There is no face

They don't know that

I'm nothing without it

28. LIFE GOES ON

In the bedroom

The smell of nicotine blends well

With the streetlights below

Like the marijuana

With decaying record sleeves

Outside

Streets and sidewalks bear the weight

Of leaders, followers, outcasts

All hastily travelling

To the same hole in the ground

On the screens

Cheap imitations of a life

Sell out at bargain prices

For they promise eternal happiness

And too much is never enough

Inside

Sobriety takes on double meanings

As addicts tighten vices

Loosen morals

And smoke pipe dreams

29. GONE

The cushions miss you

They rest on sofas and chairs

Upright and untouched

The basement misses you

Unreachable places you once explored

Will gather cobwebs once again

The windows miss you

Ever-generous with their sunbeams

Warming only the floor

Our clothes miss you

On them were pieces of you

Now they hang, too clean

Our laps miss you

They were all beds to you

And so, for you, we refused to move

We miss you

It's too quiet

You're not at your place at the table

30. KEEP RUNNING

There is sanctuary

Just beyond the horizon

Don't let me lose you

Keep running

If we keep running

We can reach it

But should you lose me

Keep running

* 9 7 8 9 3 5 8 7 3 8 7 4 2 *